ORTHODOX ICON COLORING BOOK

— VOL. 8 —

13 Icons of the Saints

SIMON OSKOLNIY

Printed in the United States of America

CONTENTS

СИМО
ОНЪ
МИХА
ИЛЪ

ГАВРИ
ИЛЪ

Plate 1.
St. Nicholas — 19th century
by Anonymous

Plate 2.
Saint Zosima and Savvatiy Solovetskie — 19th century
by Anonymous

Plate 3.
Saint Anastasia — 16th century
by Anonymous

Plate 4.
St. George and Dragon — 19th century
by Anonymous

Plate 5.

St. Vasiliy John Grigoriy — 19th century

by Anonymous

Plate 6.
Saint Theodore — 19th century
by Anonymous

Plate 7.
St. Nicholas Rescues Ship — 19th century
by Anonymous

Plate 8.
St. Nicholas — 19th century
by Anonymous

Plate 9.

St. John — 16th century

by Anonymous

Plate 10.
St. Dmitriy Solunskiy — 19th century
by Anonymous

Plate 11.
St. Artemiy — 18th century
by Anonymous

Plate 12.
St. John Evangelist — 17th century
by Anonymous

Plate 13.
St. Pyatnitsa — 16th century
by Anonymous

www.ingramcontent.com/pod-product-compliance
Lightning Source LLC
Chambersburg PA
CBHW081235020426
42331CB00012B/3181
* 9 7 8 1 6 1 9 4 9 5 5 5 5 *